This book is dedicated with love to my dear sister, who taught me how to make this dream a reality. She sent me on a scavenger hunt that was out of the norm; showed me what I already had inside but was too distracted to reach. In that scavenger hunt, I found love for myself that's been stored because I was so busy loving everyone else; I found beauty that was hidden behind stress, and most of all I found me.

Thank you, Edna!

A Codger

I met a codger some time ago
and thought he could be tamed,
but he was so flagitious
was no wonder he was unclaimed.

His odor was horribly alliaceous
he kept himself at bay;
maybe it was because at night
by trashcans he would lay.

He carried this thing, framboesia,
a contagious tropical disease;
it was on his face and genitals
resembling fruit like strawberries.

This codger also had ataxia,
which made him walk a little funny;
people would often stare and laugh
so he stayed hidden when it was sunny.

Had I known he was all these things
I would have walked the other way;
but now I know his weaknesses
so I guess I'll have to stay.

A Lonely Woman

I met a man down at the Western Palloon
with one look he caught my eye.
I took a seat in the corner booth,
a lonely woman was I.

He sat down, tipped his hat and said,
"whatever you're drinking I'll buy".
His eyes were drifting back and forth,
a lonely woman was I.

I felt as though I had walked for days
and miles while trying to hitch a ride
I couldn't be happier to get a free drink
a lonely woman was I.

He bought the drink and I took a sip
then carried me to his room to lie
As he climbed on top, I whispered
If you touch me, you will die.

A Woman's Worth

Cautiously I pen this write
with unbearable weight on my heart.
If it weren't for personal experiences,
I would not know where to start.

Fragmenting a woman's virtue
branding fear in her fragile mind,
robbing her of the one thing
that usually makes a man go blind.

This darkened rage within his eyes,
was it in his heart at birth?
Or was he not taught her value
and more importantly, a woman's worth.

We are more than the gold you see
between our platinum thighs.
A woman's worth, invaluable,
please wake up and recognize.

ABC's of a Nation Divided, The

I have never heard as much mentioned
about the KKK, the ABC's and XYZ's.
These are very frightening times people,
hug your neighbor and smile, please.

We can stand for a purpose
or run like Forrest Gump;
divided we are defeated
by a dictator with a lump.

A lump on his thumb
because he can't stop tweeting.
America, it is now time for
a town-hall impeachment meeting.

A lump on his head
causing him to say outrageous stuff.
Wake up, rise up America
stand against hatred, enough is enough.

We have a man running our nation
that is not fit to be leading,
Let's do something before it is too late
I am begging and I am pleading.

Beautifully Woven Festoon

Underneath the light
I crawl into bed;
after a yawn and a stretch
I lay down my head.

Hoping to fall asleep
and dream a dream,
but I toss and I turn
most of the night, it seem.

I repositioned myself
so I could see the moon,
watch its beaming light
on the stars bestrewn.

Sometimes they tell a story,
the stars when they shine;
when it's quiet you can hear
and see each angel align.

Spelling out your name
adding an angelic tune;
so sweet the sound
beautifully woven festoon.

Bemused

Bemused by my inability to rationalize
sequential events leading me to this day,
and how so much in so little time materialize
is only a vivid image due to a fog that gets in the way.

So I find a peaceful place to release a sigh
that can be heard miles and miles away
echoing relief as I gather shards of memories,
mostly bad ones that caused my heart to decay.

From an early age, discipline and silence,
speak when spoken to, shut up and obey;
mom chain-smoked while watching Soaps
and dad claimed he had to work every holiday.

Sadly I live in seclusion to eschew conflict
with those I love so dearly this very day,
those whose ears hear only what they want
instead of seeing the love and hope I try to convey.

Change is Good

I can be changed
by what happens to me
but I refuse to be reduced by it.

I can accept change
and put in the necessary work
it will take to conform to it.

I can be changed
by conforming to change
allowing my heart to prosper from it.

Change is good
creating something new;
it works for me
and it can work for you.

Contradiction Causes Pain

Listening to what you said today,
something just didn't sound right;
the story you told of what happened
was totally different than last night.

Immuned to the truth you've become,
telling lie, after lie, to the next;
leaving no one to believe in you
trust is out of the window, perplexed.

Stranger than fiction as you fabricate
the truth hidden between the lies you tell;
causing an uproar within your mind
rotting your brain with a horrible smell.

Your friends can smell it a mile away
knowing a lie is about to be told;
straighten up, stop exaggerating the truth
walk proud, stand tall, be honest and bold.

Overstating and bending the truth can be
the worse addiction of twisted words;
bringing pain to the those you love,
closing the door where love brews, stirs.

Cookies

Oatmeal with raisins
or sugar with cinnamon sprinkles?
Too much of a bad thing
can give you unwanted wrinkles.

My all-time favorite
are those good 'ol chocolate chips.
I once ate too many not thinking
of what it'd do to my hips.

As hard as it was
to remove them off my hips,
I try even harder
to keep them away from my lips.

Oatmeal, sugar with sprinkles,
chocolate chip, or macadamia nut,
cookies are no longer my friend
because they're no good for my butt.

Dear God,,,

May I please have a moment
of your precious time?
Is it okay if I come to you;
some things are weighing heavily on my mind.

There are so many things
I want to thank you for;
certainly I don't pause enough
to give thanks with my knees to the floor.

Lost and alone in a universe so big
I'm reaching for your hand;
please walk with me, guide me
to happier souls in your land.

Everyone here is so uptight and stressed;
they seem to have forgotten how to smile.
Remind them happiness is the way and is
the only thing needed to grace their style.

I also want to say I love you for blessing
my mind, my spirit, my fingers, and my pen;
thank you for giving me a good heart
and an ability to express what's deep within.

Devil That Lives Inside, The

Blame it on multiple personalities,
I say it's just plain evil lust.
The fact that she was in my house,
tell me, why should I even trust.

Trust that she was here to dust,
wash the windows and scrub the shower.
When knowing I did some cleaning myself,
it shouldn't have taken more than an hour.

What is it that makes us want to cheat,
a behavior that's never justified.
That hunger, thirst, devious craving
all comes from the devil that lives inside.

Rebuke that fool, don't let him in.
Remember what the Bible says about sin?
Sorry to say, but neither do I.
But I do know it resides in the wandering eye.

Inside each and every one of us
is a Dr. Jekyl and Mr. Hyde.
Which do you choose to let control
the devil that lives inside?

Echoes Beneath The Stairs

With replications of my mind
reading my dreams in a soft whisper
echoing the sound of footprints
of bloody sand leading to the stairs

thus reveled, making resound chants
of beautiful noises, but contained
such a fool am I, never satisfied,
yearning to hear the fainting vocals

inside a crawlspace so small
you can feel the reverberation
of the cobwebs and whispers
sound reflections obstructing

the echoes beneath the stairs,
daunting to say the least, the space
where the sun doesn't shine
underneath the stairs, I hear echoes.

Etched

I was going to leave you
...then the stars did shine
but my heart always knew
...they never did in mine

filled with deep darkness
...I trotted to get to tunnel's end
midway through I saw a glow
...so my hand I did extend

but somehow you drifted
...further into the black hole
taking with you my breath
...I'm no longer feeling whole

so I have to leave you
...like the stars do the skies
this story that we drew
...never saw my eyes

back to the drawing board
...to where we were a sketch
beginning with eyes meeting eyes
...creating love, etch by etch

Etched 2...

*I was going to leave you
...then the stars did shine
stole your heart under the moon
...a kiss so gently to make you mine*

*giving in to love's first kiss
...we made promises to be true
my heart took a chance
...on being loved by you*

*you broke your promise
...not long after that first kiss
so I decided to walk away
...when you made my eyes mist*

*the day I left you
...my day turned to night
even through my tears
...I knew my decision was right*

*praying as I walked away
...not for me, but for you
for God to have mercy
...to help you make it through*

*back to the drawing board
...to where we once were a sketch
we took things slow, and in time
...love was created, etch by etch*

Family

Family begins and ends with heart,
you have to thrive on it to have it;
not necessarily meaning a blood connect
and doesn't mean it has to be perfect.

The definition of family has a thin line
around being born into and adopted into.
I have lots of adopted family in my life
to take up the slack from sibling strife.

Anyone willing to wrap their arms around me
when they can see I am in pain or down,
taking notice that I'm feeling hurt
and not turning away kicking up dirt.

My many sisters and brothers,
through Christ, are my fam
for they treat me like I'm gold
and accept me for who I am.

Five Years A Slave

I put my heart into loving you;
at the time it seemed the right thing to do.
Blood, sweat, and tears so freely I gave;
for the next five years I worked like a slave.

Got dressed up put on make-up, too;
it wasn't done for me, I did it all for you.
You never even noticed you never looked twice;
I got dolled up hoping you would say something nice.

Neither red lipstick nor a nighty with lace
could turn you on or put a smile on your face.
You were supposed to love me back,
but that heart of yours is cold and black.

No longer is it your love I crave;
I give up after being five years a slave.

Four Hundred-Sixty Five

What number did you have on your gurney?
Hers was four-hundred and sixty-five.
That number represents her blood sugar;
It's a miracle she is still alive.

Inflicting millions of people every day
there is a name for this disease;
silently creeps into you without warning
this life-changer is called diabetes.

We were informed of her diagnosis
when she was the young age of ten;
for the next eleven years, it's been
pins and needles, needles and pins.

Each times she goes into D.K.A.
she is one step closer to death.
We both have the same fear,
the day she takes her last breath.

Bravery may have lost the battle,
but hope is still alive.
If we don't give up the fight,
we will love, live, and survive.

God Loves Me

God...

L~et's me make mistakes
O~ver and over again.
V~ocally I pray, knowing
E~phemeral I would be without His
S~empiternal love for

Me...

Guilty Until Proven Innocent

Accused of a heinous act
his claim of innocence unheard;
convicted without gathering every fact
what happens next is absurd.

Judged by a jury of his peers,
does that mean same age or race?
Peers or a jury of prejudice folks
taking advantage of deciding his fate.

Falsely accused, no one could predict
he'd be sentenced and put on death row;
given a flagitious number to depict
an injection giving him a fatal blow.

Undeserving of this grievous burden
never giving up the fight of his life;
searched and found a group of lawyers
that fought to get him back to his wife.

Never giving up and embracing his truth
exoneration came at a pace that was slow;
holding the love of his life once again
pardoned and released from death row.

Heart on Loan

I always knew when I was a child
someday I would become a woman, grown;
it never occurred to me, as an adult,
I would have to put my heart on loan.

A man once came up to me
and asked how much he had to pay
for a night out on the town
if he put my heart on lay-a-way.

Another man soon approached
looking muscular, handsome and strong
and said if he gave me his salary
would I allow him to come along.

He noted the journey, however long
whether physical or by telephone;
he asked if it was at all possible
to put my love and my heart on loan.

Here to Stay

Skin hair, a pimple, and maybe acne, too,
are things I would be if given the chance;
removing them is nothing compared to a kiss
to a song that makes me want to dance.

The chills my touch gave you, was your hair
dancing on your skin, tickling your soul
from head to toe breathlessly I sigh,
for now I am yours, you have total control.

Take of my flesh and do as you please,
I chose not a thing of that which you lack;
a picking of somethings you can get rid of
that are sure to keep coming back.

You are my bag of legacies
and I am here to stay;
our hearts will be dancing forever
warmth will remain, where we lay.

Honorary Degree

When all is said and done
we choose the path in which we walk;
It is our prime words selection
coming out of our mouths when we talk.

When we speak in elegant tone
with an exquisite body frame,
not pertaining to fat or skinny
but the personification we proclaim.

College is not necessary
to earn this Honorary Degree;
when all is said and done,
we plant the seed we want to be.

Hot Soup and a Blister

I was heading to my house
with a cup of hot soup
distracted, stepped on a rock
and tripped on a stoop.

Thought I was okay
so I kept on going;
I burned my left hand
without even knowing.

Wanna know how I knew?
I felt this burning kind of pain
so I looked and saw a swelling blister
then lost it, went insane.

So I got to the house
and knocked on the door.
mom saw the blistered hand
and fainted to the floor.

I Belong

It's no ordinary miracle you blew into my path
taking my heart by storm;
you've blown through an unfamiliar territory
strangely out of the norm.

My last tornado left a gaping exit wound
I caved without conviction;
wading in the open waters and I drank,
which caused an addiction.

You gave all my extremities a whirlwind
of love, blow by blow,
twist by twist, with your cloud of perfection
rains of terror, you know.

I tried to take shelter, shield my heart, but
you were so strong;
surviving your grip, I now realize it is
in your twister, I belong.

I Surrender

I've known for years
I couldn't do it alone,
which is why I should have
trusted the man on the throne.

I've learned my lesson
and I've learned it well,
to surrender, concede all
to God's personnel.

No longer will I
try to go it alone;
I will call Him up
and hear a heavenly tone.

Laying it all out,
my hardships, on the table;
He put it in writing,
I'm willing, and I'm able.

Imprinting Love

When I look at you, gazingly,
I see a twinkle in your mind.
Imprinting love in my heart
you are an uncommon find.

Not only a diamond in the rough
but that of topaz and pearl
with a sparkle in your eyes,
....blushing like a schoolgirl.

By my side, promise you will stay.
Leave your footprints `cross my heart
as if crossing the open sky ensuring,
always together, never apart.

Between the twinkle in your mind
and promises we will never be apart,
you are the brightest star hovering over the moon
imprinting a permanent smile in my heart.

Let's Talk

Serenity is what I seek, oh Lord
I have come to You for advice.
It is with conviction before You I stand
on Your heavenly paradise.

I need to know what I can do
to help a nation so divided;
help us all love one another
share the land You have provided.

I am listening with an open heart
watching with a sightful eye;
easily blinded by all the hate
so it is Your name I glorify.

Love Stinks

Love gives you a reason to love,
and in that deceitful generosity
it invades your heart plaguing it
in epic proportions, reaching monstrosity.

That moment of infatuation
making your heart feel fully loaded,
ready to take on what you think is love,
is not enough time to prepare you
for what's about to be unloaded.

You see, love is not a silent killer
on the contrary, you take hit after hit
getting pounded by waves of fallaciousness
that raises a high stakes doubt,
I've been there, too, I must admit.

That doubt is clearly not enough.
Infatuation is pulling your strings.
Your emotions are in a tug of war,
Walk away, don't walk away, (repeat)
The hurt is like a dagger on springs.

Although love is a reason to love in itself,
it is brutal and often time stinks,
I want it all, the good, the bad, and the ugly
regardless what anyone else thinks.

Love That Dare Not Speak Its Name, The

The love that dare not speak its name
is one far, in between, and few.
The love I have taught me things,
a new way of expressing my point of view.

She taught me there was no love
without a little bit of pain;
she said it wasn't possible to have a day
without a night, or clouds without rain.

She said that if I trust in her heart
and believe in all that which is above,
I will have blessings in abundance
in the form of a wife, a child, and love.

It is a myth to me that God is a man.
All that I have learned about Him,
I find in this specimen they call a woman.
She is my jewel, my rock, my gem.

It was in all she did to me and for me,
that made us love the same;
she gave of herself copiously
in a love that dare not speak its name.

Mom's Buttery Biscuits

She made the best homemade biscuits,
buttery and glazed with a touch of honey.
Mom spent most of her time in the kitchen,
it was the room that was always sunny.

She didn't mind washing the dishes, in fact,
I heard her say it made her fingernails grow.
The milk she drank made them very strong,
so she used them to help pluck the crow.

Never knew it was crow, always thought it was chicken
smothered with grilled onions in a hearty gravy;
nevertheless, made sure she cooked more than enough
to feed the nearby soldiers that were in the navy.

To this day, I can smell those hot buttery biscuits
that my mother slaved in the kitchen to make;
the warm, soft, and buttery taste to the last crumb
was such a sweet treat, she never had to bake cake.

My Best Friend

We became acquainted six years ago
through a chance meet;
sometimes you wanted me to give you ice
other times you wanted to feel heat

Through the eyes looking back at me
there was no indication you were there;
you became more and more prevalent
requiring the maximum amount of care

Just as our relationship grew fonder
your love for me was no match;
I could not keep up with your growth
when one flew the coup, another would hatch

Joint to joint, bone to bone,
the competition had nothing to gain;
when you can't beat 'em, join 'em
my best friend, my confidante, my pain.

Nightmare Screams

You will not find me in a cloud
of hand-me-down dreams,
but you may find me deep
in your nightmare screams.

The love I once gave you
that put a smile on your face,
was stolen by another
leaving you with a tear trace.

Your friend called to tell me
you weren't doing too well;
had the nerve to say I'm the reason
your life is now a living hell.

She also said that when you sleep
you awake with nightmare screams;
babbling something about a cloud
and hand-me-down dreams.

No Shoes, No Shirt, No Service

Walking alongside the mountainous trail
Searching for myself, looking for clues
In the darkness blanketed by a starlit sky
I must have been sleepwalking, no shoes.

My mind is missing in the fog,
In a haze, I'm dazed, lost and hurt
Standing along the hill of an avalanche
Freezing all alone and cold, no shirt.

Life has failed me, let me down
Leaving me discombobulated, nervous
I stumbled into cafe hope
Was handed a ticket that read, no service.

Planted

Creating a heavenly paradise
was not a leisurely task for me;
planted the seed when I was younger
using the platform of a knowledge tree.

I knew early on I was destined to have
my piece of the Promised Land.
It was not an option to abnegate
the fruit God planted in my hand.

The biggest seed of financial strength
giving not riches, but freedom planted
has been difficult to reach, unattainable.
I need a genie with one wish left to be granted.

My wish would be to have my Garden of Eden,
and a few bags of seeds I can plant,
trees that at full growth will have
the face of Ulysses S. Grant.

Quiet Please

Shhh!
Can't you see
I am trying to read?
It's not just any book,
so I beg and I plead.

Hush!
You will hear sweet music
coming out of my mouth?
Can you hear the soft whisper
I learned from down south.

Silence!
Silence is deemed to be golden,
a library of magical treasures;
listen and feel my spoken words
let the music satisfy your pleasures.

Quiescence!
Sparkling eyes makes my heart jump
To the beat of every word I read;
I believe what my grandma told me,
"I have to read to succeed".

Real Beauty

The power of beauty
is the sword within its smile;
skin deep they say it is
but you're valued by grace and style.

If a man's vibration is to beauty,
what does the heart do?
If his eyes gaze at flawless skin,
within is not what he sees in you.

Accept not lust over thirst,
starve a cold, feed a fever;
it's not until you feel the hunger pangs
that you become a true believer.

Make him want to work
for what is to come, not the pay;
show him it is appreciated
at the end of each and every day.

So many ways to say thank you,
I think you know what I mean.
There is no need for detail
but privately, can be obscene.

Reboot

So, we tell ourselves there's no way out,
the only thing that makes sense, is to stay;
being forced with antagonizing threats,
leaving us feeling that we are the prey.

"Please don't leave", is what her eyes reads,
but you'd have to be looking at them to know;
screaming, "Mom, please come back",
strange things happens when he closes the doe.

Keeping my family at bay, no one ever knew
an escape route was needed, I wanted out;
unwanted spam from all the tears I've cried
but today I cry no more, I'm about to logout.

The only way to rid this virus is to reboot,
needing to clear the cache and erase all history;
I'm not talking a restart, but a total shutdown;
source identified, a solution's no longer a mystery.

Sacrifice or Love

So many times have I heard a parent say,
"I made all those sacrifices for my child".
If working twelve hours every single day
is a sacrifice, I am totally beguiled.

I say this because I did the same
the whole "put a roof over their head, whereof";
the difference between you and I is,
I looked at it as being nothing but love.

Did I give up a few things for them, yes;
I skipped a couple pair of jeans and shoes.
Giving birth meant I no longer came first
and I forfeited my right to choose.

I may have gone to bed hungry, only I,
still not a sacrifice but love unconditional.
The way I see it, not to say that it is wrong,
parenting today is very nontraditional.

Silicone Soul

Seduced by the moon and equatorial sun
our encounter was **indubitably contrived**.
Who was I to **castigate** this **tatterdemalion**?
My visual perception compromised, revived.

Your **obstreperous** and **truculent** conduct
became more prevalent with time,
giving nullification to the **dalliance**
dismissing you before investing a dime.

Erudite describes your discernment as
inexplicable **annals** and **abhorrent**,
not to mention your **virulent** tendencies
with **prosaic** words of **amorphic** extent.

It didn't take long to figure you out
and see through your sweet talking **trope**;
life has taught me to listen to my intuition
to avoid a **stentorian** hanging with my own rope.

*The words in bold represent the words to contrive this poem.

Silken Waters

When I asked you to love, honor, and obey me,
you went a step further; gave me twin daughters.
From that one question you changed my world;
I'm reminded when I pray above the silken waters.

For these gifts you gave willingly and unselfishly,
your love and my love are united as one, together.
We are the lightening sunshine; thunderous torch;
the burning soul inside each other's heart forever.

There is no bridge that could ever keep us apart,
now that we are a family, and because you said yes.
I will do all to protect your heart, and love you;
remembering that I am loved, and I am blessed.

For when I asked you to love, honor, and obey me,
you said yes and gave me a family with twin daughters.
Uniting our souls together and forever as one;
on the golden bridge, high above the silken waters.

Stand Still

Happiness is an affectional feeling
that gets you all worked up;
it is everyone's desire to have
a bit of it, in their little cup.

The problem is once we get it,
rationale is diminished, thrown out;
leaving us to contend with heartache
and emptiness, filled only with doubt.

Happiness plays games and tricks
on the heart and on the mind;
abandoning smiles and laughter
one step, one day, at a time.

So here's what I say should
happiness find you, which it will,
welcome it with open arms,
slow down, breathe, stand still.

Stay

Should I stay or should I go,
the question burning in my mind.
The answer should be easy;
words from your mouth no longer kind.

We used to love on each other
our thing was to laugh and play;
breathing in each other's breath
even when life was in disarray.

Completing each other's sentences
we wouldn't have it no other way;
yesterday you said you wanted to go,
today I am asking you to stay.

Embrace the change we'd have to make;
I have something I want you to know.
Those things I said, I didn't mean;
I want you to stay, please don't go.

Stay Gold

Mother never told me
to put sex on hold;
she never told me
I should stay gold.

I can vaguely remember
she spoke of a silver lining;
something about being a lady
that later would be defining.

Mother never said much
just let me do as I please;
when all I wanted was for her
to put her arms on me and squeeze.

I didn't know love then
the way I know love today;
I had a few propositions
where I should have walked away.

Because I didn't walk away
escaping a world so dark and cold,
I have three beautiful children
in my life I tell to stay gold.

Still Voices

Still voices can be incredibly loud,
especially when used to convey an emotion.
Consider tears of joy, tears of sadness,
eyes closed, hands raised during devotion.

Close your eyes and use your imagination
putting yourself in what I said above;
were you able to feel the sadness,
did you feel God's unchanging love?

Silence is golden largely because of faith.
Spirituality (spirit) is a silent belief
known throughout the world, however,
individually we pray for solace and relief.

On the flip side, silence can hurt
those unspoken words of "I love you"
can't magically heal a broken heart,
but "I'm sorry" is always a good place to start.

It's those times when we need noise
to feel, understand, renew love,,, feed;
feed your hunger to feel renewed love
understand this is a right,,, this is a need.

Storm Chaser, The

In the pursuit of happiness
we are often chasing dreams;
going after the ultimate prize
is sometimes harder than it seems.

Into a deep and shallow trench we fall
while on our quest for immortality;
furrow soil turning into quicksand
immobilizing us by the storm of morality.

The hurricane hits with forced winds
stirring any and all rational thinking
followed by torrential rains, therefore
into the quicksand, we are sinking.

Life takes us all by storm
putting us in a path of danger;
the decision to rise or fall
will be the deciding game changer.

Sunlight Wine

The crescent moon
has an amazing shape
and got its blood color
from the juice of a grape.

I prayed to the Gods
before I sat down to dine
for the heavens to quench my thirst
with a glass of sunlight wine.

A little on the dry side
but ever so dark and sweet;
so sweet I will buy the bottle
and finish it on my loveseat.

If wine is sunlight held together by water,
the grapes are the rain giving wine its color.

Tea Anyone?

Inside my attic beyond the dust
I share space with my friend mouse;
I often share a cup of tea
with the previous owners of the house.

I really don't mind sharing the space
because it was theirs before it was mine;
she was battling a substance addiction
his best friend was strawberry wine.

It's funny having conversations with ghosts
you'll see they are harmless at best;
be nice to them, they'll be nice to you
make them feel like welcomed guests.

Think of how a dog smells your fear
well, ghost can smell it too;
don't be afraid, invite them in
to share your attic with you.

The One In Charge

*Spending time with oneself
doesn't necessarily mean
spending time alone;
stood in a room full of people
and no one ever spoke,
as if I was unknown.*

*It wasn't, however, until recently
that I learned to get
in touch with my mind;
pain had consumed every inch of me
crippling my thoughts, my happiness,
and robbing me blind.*

*Once back in touch with my mind,
my thoughts were broadened
and happiness was found;
it no longer mattered of a conversation,
in a boardroom of people, where to me,
silence was sound.*

*Now my thoughts are simply a breeze
passing through quicker,
by far and by large;
loving the new me I have become
while on this journey realizing,
I am the one in charge.*

Tracks of My Tears

I can't help but be reminded
of the pain I have felt for years
both physical and emotional
creating the tracks of my tears.

Often feeling there's no light
at the end of the tunnel;
problems constantly mounting
in an ever whirling funnel.

Always welcoming the rain
to hide those awful tracks
starting to leave wrinkles
those ugly facial cracks.

Until one day I decided
that I would cry no more;
dry these tears forever and
bring back that smile I once wore.

I know it is waiting for me
right around that winding turn,
happiness and the smile
I have forever yearned.

True

I miss those days when we were smitten
and love was raw beyond compare;
when every beat of my heart was rhythmic to yours
inseparable, we were quite the pair.

Giving you a run for your money,
every dollar was well spent;
not on fine dining and expensive jewelry
but on a proud woman trying to represent.

While being sprung out on your love
I was being blinded by the truth,
that there was a hole in your heart
put there by someone named Ruth.

She must have hurt you awfully bad,
no matter what I did, just could not get in;
I knocked, and I knocked, and I knocked,
but the pain was locked deep within.

I don't know if I will ever feel love again
the way I felt love with you;
even though it was beautiful and short-lived,
it was a love I thought was true.

Voice, The

It speaks articulate thoughts
spinning words on a turntable
making sounds that moves your feet
and has your body shakingly unstable.

It cries reacting to fear and pain
eyes sweating and noses, rivers of slime;
someone steal me a box of tissues,
oh, I forgot, stealing is a crime.

It laughs with giggles galore
chuckling songs of a haha and glee;
the spirit is lifted with each jiggle
also giving you a spirit that is free.

When the voice is quiet and silent,
it is speaking through the mind;
silent screams, cries, and laughter, too
sounds of multiple emotions combined.

What is Knowledge?

Knowledge guides us down a path.
that is sometimes never ending;
We pray for strength and another step
in a direction that is clearly ascending.

When it seems our mind is playing tricks
and our heart is unsure which way to go,
know that this rainbow world is at your feet;
use the colors as a guide, and you will know.

Life promises us nothing, nothing at all,
it is up to you to put forth effort, commit;
putting in the work to get to that place
above the realms of possibility and not quit.

Despite our handicaps, which we all have,
we are capable of the function to strive.
Reach for the stars, infinity and beyond
making only decisions that help us arrive.

Who, What, When, Why

Who we are in a life without purpose,
makes us create a phantom meaning.
In this quest to understand ourselves,
it is the lies of gravity in which we are leaning.

What lies we tell, hiding the truth that we feel
like worthless menaces to a large society,
not totally uneducated but don't know how
to obtain and maintain insobriety.

When we lie to keep up with the Joneses,
unknowingly and secretly they, too, are lying.
With honest living, riches will come if we
don't forget whose name we should be glorifying.

Why we cannot put a price on life,
we are all worth so much more than we think.
The answers we all seek will come
once we get our trust and faith in sync.

What's In a Name?

Elegant as can be
when she speaks
she displays
eloquent techniques

Delightful of a sort
with a beautiful smile
melting hearts with warmth,
with grace, and with style

Necessary in my life
always by my side
keeping me close to her heart
with arms open wide

Authentic and down to earth
health conscious and wise
constantly pushing me
to eat good and exercise

I am a much better person
with inspiration overflowing
I have my sister Edna to thank,
so my thanks to her, I'm bestowing!

A Codger	God Loves Me
A Lonely woman	Guilty Until Proven Innocent
A Woman's Worth	Heart on Loan
ABC's of a Nation Divided	Here to Stay
Beautifully Woven Festoon	Honorary Degree
Bemused	Hot Soup and a Blister
Change is Good	I Belong
Contradiction Causes Pain	I Surrender
Cookies	Imprinting Love
Dear God	Let's Talk
Devil that Lives Inside, The	Love Stinks
Echoes Beneath the Stairs	Love that Dare Not Speak,,,
Etched	Mom's Buttery Biscuits
Etched 2	My Best Friend
Family	Nightmare Screams
Five Years a Slave	No Shoes, No Shirt, No Servic
Four Hundred-Sixty Five	Planted

Quiet Please
Real Beauty
Reboot
Sacrifice or Love
Silicone Soul
Silken Waters
Stand Still
Stay
Stay Gold

Still Voices
Storm Chaser, The
Sunlight Wine
Tea Anyone
The One in Charge
Tracks of My Tears
True
Voice, The
What is Knowledge?
Who, What, When, Why

About the author,

The Woman I Am

The character in me allows me to see
The beauty of life each day that I awake
It finds a way for me to make someone smile
Even when sometimes there's a lot at stake

I am the woman I am and that woman is me!

The devoted woman in me allows me to be,
For greatness aspired, for learning inspired
And for everything else I'm supposed to be
On my knees to a higher power

I am the woman I am and that woman is me!

The woman of strength in me
Have and will continue to weather any storm
With no shortage of hope
For God has given me the will, the courage,
and the strength to cope

I am a woman of character, devotion,
and strength you see;
I am the woman I am
and the woman I want to be.

My name is Linda M Johnson, born and raised in Southern California, the 5th of seven children. Other books I have published include: true love comes from The Heart, the Heart of a Woman, as well as a couple of children books dedicated to my granddaughters, Saniyah and Marlee.

Please visit MyPoetryKitchen. I'm sure you'll find something in my pantry to feed your soul. If you're considering leaving a tip, please do so in the form of subscribing. I would love to hear from you. Thank you very much for your support.

Email:
LindaMJ@mypoetrykitchen.com
airfrcmom@msn.com

Social:
Youtube/myvoiceination
Instagram/airfrcmom
Pinterest/airfrcmom

Made in the USA
Middletown, DE
05 March 2023

26268708R00038